D1406420

Boardsailing in waves

Boardsailing in waves

Dave Cordell
photographs by David Edmund-Jones

Fernhurst Books

Contents

Acknowledgements

Thanks are due to Tony Lavender of Ilford Films Ltd and Peter Joel of Pan Am for their invaluable assistance in the preparation of this book.

©Fernhurst Books 1984

First published 1984 by Fernhurst Books, 13 Fernhurst Road, London SW6 7JN

All rights reserved. No part of the publication may be reproduced, stored in a retrieval system, or transmitted in any form or by any means, electronic, mechanical, photocopying, recording or otherwise, without the prior permission of the publishers.

ISBN 0 906754 15 1

Composition by A & G Phototypesetters, Knaphill
Printed by Ebenezer Baylis & Son Ltd, Worcester

Part 1
Sailing in waves

1 Rigging

It's been a long, hot drive to the beach, the wind's force 5 and the water's blue and inviting. What's more natural than to sling the rig together, launch right by the car park and get sailing straight away?

Try to resist the temptation! If the board and sail are badly rigged it will spoil your day's sailing. At best the gear will behave badly and at worst you'll find yourself retying ropes at sea or having to come ashore to make adjustments.

So let's start by having a look at how to set up your equipment for maximum performance on the water.

Footstraps

Footstraps are designed to keep you on the board — whether you're punching out through the surf or doing a tip-dip. It follows that they should fit your feet properly, and not come undone except under extreme load.

Decide whether you're going to sail with bare feet or wear shoes. Then adjust each strap so it covers the area just behind your toes. If the strap is looser than this your foot may get caught when you wipe out — nasty if you're under the sail. But your feet will come out of tight straps too easily — choosing, of course, the worst moment to do so. It's embarrassing to find yourself attached to the board only by your toenails in the middle of a jump.

If you have safety release straps which pop open under pressure, test them by giving each one a good pull with your hands. If it comes open then it's much too easily opened — in the middle of a jump there will be far more pressure on them than that — so adjust accordingly.

Retracting daggerboards

If you're sailing a long board with a retracting dagger, wash out sand and stones from the case before you set sail and make sure you can adjust the dagger easily with your foot. There's nothing worse than kicking at the handle when the case is gummed up or the dagger is just plain stiff.

Skegs

A good set of skegs is essential to a board's performance. They must be positioned properly, and be the right length, stiffness, shape and finish. We will look at skegs in more detail in Part 2 — for the moment, make sure that your skegs fit tightly in the skeg box, i.e. there is no side-to-side slop. If there is, tape along each skeg's base and refit into the box.

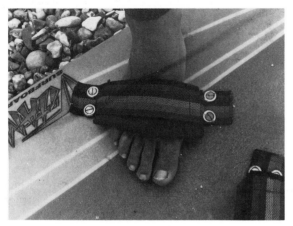

Left: a correctly adjusted footstrap covers the area just behind the toes. Right: wave jumping makes enormous demands on rig and board.

Which sail?

Once you've checked the board over, the next job is to choose the right sail for the day's conditions.

Ideally (though not everyone can afford it!) you should have several sails so you can cope with every windstrength on the Beaufort scale — from force 0 to 7 or above. These will range from a big 7.5 m² (75 sq.ft) sail for light winds to a pocket-handkerchief 3.0 m² (30 sq.ft). For high-wind sailing you can get by with three sails — 4.2 m² (40 sq.ft), 4.9 m² (50 sq.ft) and 5.6 m² (55 sq.ft).

A rough way of checking is to rig up near the water and test the sail on the beach. If it's too big you'll be thrown around when you sheet in. If it's too small you'll sheet in and fall backwards. It will be OK if you can sheet in (with effort) and hold it,

leaning away from the sail with the strength of the wind holding you up.

Look also at what is happening on the water. Is the wind consistent, dropping, increasing or gusting? (Gusts are shown by darker patches moving over the water.) Modify your sail choice accordingly.

The sail selector chart below may help you. It's easiest to use if you have a small anemometer and can average out the wind values over a five minute period. Alternatively the local weather station or sailing club should have details on the day's forecast. The chart shows that for a sailor of average weight in 35 knots of wind a 3.5 m² (35 sq.ft) sail is ideal, and so on. If you don't have the chart with you the magic number to remember is 70: if the wind is blowing 25 knots, 70 − 25=45

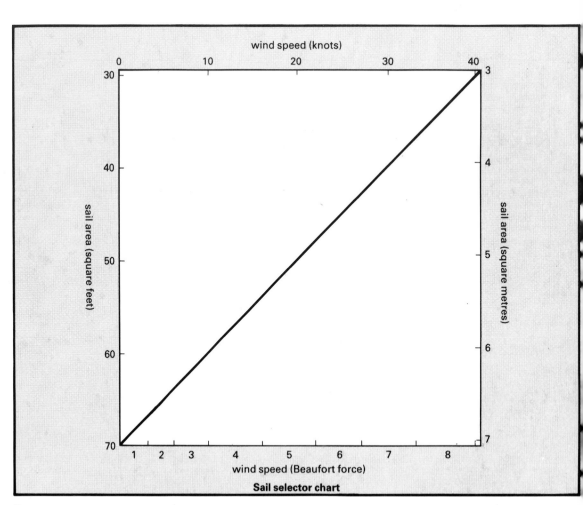

Sail selector chart

Right: after putting the sail on the mast and fitting the universal joint, apply slight pressure to the downhaul. Below: tie the inhaul around the mast at forehead height.

so use a 45 sq.ft sail. Of course heavier sailors can use a somewhat larger sail in a given wind while lightweights will have to use something smaller.

Despite all this, experience on the water is really the best way to learn what your sails will do in various wind strengths.

Having chosen your sail, the next step is to rig it properly.

Rigging the sail and boom

1. Push the sail onto the mast, making sure the tip of the mast is located correctly at the top of the sail. Insert the battens, making sure that all creases are removed from the batten pockets. Check that the mast is long enough for the sail sleeve — at least 30 cm (about a foot) of mast should be showing at the bottom. If not, you will need a mast extension. Fit the universal joint and apply slight tension to the downhaul.

2. Tie the boom onto the mast. To gain maximum performance from the sail, the boom must be locked tight and at 90 degrees to the mast. Short booms are better for high-wind sailing and they really complement a high-clewed sail in waves. Firstly decide on the height you want your boom by holding up the mast and tying the inhaul around it at forehead height. Remember not to tie too near the top of the hole in the sail, since the hole will move down the mast when the downhaul is pulled tight. With experience you may find you want to rig the boom at a different height: if your arms are getting tired quickly they are too far above your head, so rig the boom lower. But if it is too low you won't get enough leverage, the rig will be difficult to control and your body will drag through the waves. Now place the boom above the knot and bind above and below, making sure that you have plenty of rope and that you can get your boom really rigid to the mast so

9

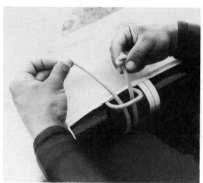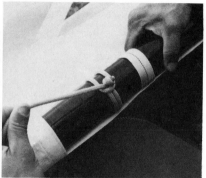

that there is no sideways movement. Tie the boom as shown in the photos; it helps if you have a mast-locating end on your boom that fits neatly around the mast.

3. Pull the outhaul (at the clew) as tight as possible. The photos show one way of doing this; alternatively get a friend to help pull the sail tight. The tighter the sail is pulled out, the flatter it will set when fully rigged. Make sure it is tied off with no loose ends. If the boom is too long for the sail (ideally it should just fit the sail when full outhaul pressure is applied) then one trick to get the sail setting flat is to tie the clew of the sail to one side of the boom: this will keep the sail really flat with no movement from side to side. An adjustable boom is the ideal answer so that all your sails fit perfectly.

4. Once the outhaul is tied off, downhaul pressure can be applied to the sleeve. A three-to-one purchase should be used to get the sail really flat. Make sure that all creases are removed from the sail especially just behind the mast sleeve itself. Once again get a friend to help tie off so that the downhaul doesn't slip.

5. If you have set your sail correctly for high-wind sailing it should be really flat with hardly any fullness showing. This is because the airflow over the sail is much stronger than over recreational sails used in lighter winds. If too much fullness is built into a high-wind sail it will become very difficult to control with the centre of effort moving backwards and forwards, turning the board up into the wind.

Top row: tying the boom to the mast. Note the way the mast is rotated to make everything really tight. Above: tying the outhaul. Opposite, centre left: lines such as the outhaul should be both cleated and tied off. Centre right: clew arrangement when the boom is too long (ideally, use an adjustable boom).
Bottom: tightening the downhaul.

10

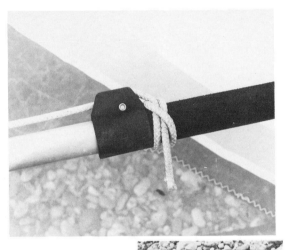
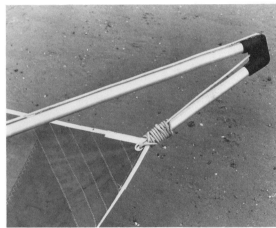

Above: badly rigged sails. On the left, the horizontal wrinkles show the downhaul is too slack; right, the outhaul should be tightened to remove the vertical

creases. Opposite: the harness lines should be rigged so your arms are just bent when sailing.
Below: a board protector.

Once you are ready, give everything one last check over, re-tie anything that looks suspect and test the wind strength on the beach. Here are some things to watch out for: the boom too high, too loose, the location on the mast tip badly worn or badly fitting, mast foot or mast extension a sloppy fit (use tape or gasket sleeve), battens inserted wrongly.

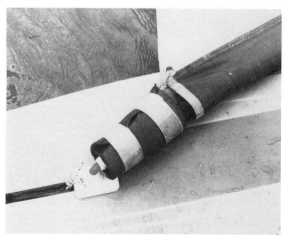

Attaching the rig to the board

When fixing your mast foot into the board make sure it is really tight. The only time you want it to come out is when you're caught in big waves or when self-rescuing. If you have a sliding mast foot, begin with the mast towards the back of the track for quicker planing ability. Sliding it right forwards will enable you to point into the wind better and also gain control in very strong gusty conditions.

For safety reasons always make a habit of tying the safety line from the *front* of the board to the mast foot swivel, especially when sailing in waves. The reason for this is that if the rig gets detached in big waves, the sail acts as an anchor and prevents the board zooming off. You will also find it easier to get board and rig back together again with the safety line rigged like this.

Board protector

Put a board protector around the base of the mast (or extension) — especially if you use a fibreglass custom board. This will stop the mast denting the deck area around the mast foot.

2 Launching in waves

It's happened to most of us at one time or another — that agonising moment as you are about to step onto your board and blast through the surf, when you realise that you have timed it badly and a muncher splats you back up the beach with your mast in a right angle. Launching in waves can be one of the trickiest parts of the day's sailing, especially when the wind is onshore. Short boards are also harder to get started than long planks. In this section I'm going to look at the technique required for both short and long boards.

Short board technique

1. Choose a part of the beach which looks inviting; aim for a cross-shore breeze, gently shelving bottom and relatively gentle waves (see wind and wave theory in part 2).

2. If the wind is very strong, set up the board and rig together and carry the whole lot down to the water's edge. This is far safer than taking them down one at a time. (I have seen many production boards blown down the beach for a considerable distance, simply because the owner had left his board broadside to the wind and had gone to fetch his rig.)

3. Check the wind direction and align the board across the wind with the mast pointing into the breeze. Pick up the board by holding onto the boom or mast and lifting the board with the front footstrap. Hold the board as close to your body as possible.

4. As you walk towards the water take a long look at what the waves are doing — are they dumping (breaking along their whole length simultaneously and crashing on the beach), are

there sets coming in with quiet times in between, are there any channels which produce flat water rips out through the break? It's always worth spending two or three minutes trying to analyse what the waves are going to do; launching at the right time and place can make things much easier. For instance if there are sets coming in, launch just after a major set has gone through.

5. To launch, walk into the water until it's knee, thigh deep (no deeper), keeping an eye on the waves coming towards you and lifting the board over them. Lower the board into a relatively flat piece of water and transfer your back hand to the boom followed by your front hand.

6. Align the board in a broad reach direction (see diagram below). With the daggerboard retracted the board will pivot about its skegs, so to turn the nose away from the wind push on the mast; pull the mast to turn the nose towards the wind.

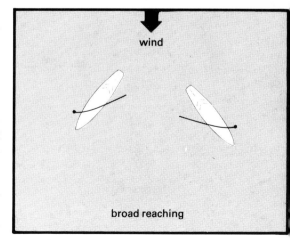

wind

broad reaching

Launching in waves can be the trickiest part of the day's sailing. The sequence below shows the method you should use to launch a short board.

Above: the author demonstrating how to launch a board that is to heavy to lift. The next problem is how to punch through the shore break (opposite). Below: Waiting for the moment to launch.

7. If possible, wait for a gust to help you accelerate away from the shore. Transfer your back foot onto the board, raise the rig so the wind helps pull you up, push off with your front leg and sheet in. Finally, lift your front foot onto the board.

8. In strong winds you will need to put your feet in the straps as soon as you step on the board. In lighter winds stand further forwards to prevent the tail sinking.

9. Sail off on a broad reach, i.e. with the waves hitting the windward rail. The whole manoeuvre is a bit like a water-start (see page 39) except you are able to stand up in the water.

Semi-floater/long board technique

If the board is too heavy to lift a different technique is needed.

1. Pick your moment, then with the board turned on edge push it through the water at 90 degress to the waves.

2. Keeping the rig above water, drop the back end of the board onto the water and quickly align it on a broad reach as described above. Then step on and sail away as for a short board. Watch out for rogue waves which slew the board round just before you step on. Don't let the board turn broadside on to the waves as this will make it difficult to start.

3   The first minute

After a successful launch into the chaos of wind and waves the next minute is critical. Your objectives are to pick up speed, negotiate the first wave and then get out through the surf as quickly as possible. Let's look first at what should happen, then what you can do if things go wrong (the diagram on page 19 shows your choices).

If everything goes right. . .

. . . you will be sailing fairly fast with your feet in the straps. As you approach the first wave, decide where is the best place to hit it, whether you want to jump, or climb it without leaving the water. I will be concentrating on jumping in a later chapter, so

let's assume you don't want 'air time' and are going to go over the wave normally. The wave will either have broken before it hits you (ugh!) or still be unbroken. In either case head for the lowest part of the wave.

Breaking water.   If you think the wave will break in front of you, or if it has already done so, bear away to pick up speed then transfer your weight to your back foot (this allows the bow to ride up over the white water). Just before you hit the wave luff

quickly into the wind so the nose of the board points to the wave — by doing this you present as little resistance as possible. Don't let your board turn broadside on to the white water otherwise you will be knocked off.

As you pass over the wave crouch down, push the board through the surf with your feet and quickly push the rig forward so that you bear away again to gather speed.

Swell. If the wave has not broken in front of you, again look for the least steep part and head for that section. If you find yourself faced with a large peak which is about to break, change direction rapidly in an attempt to reach a part of the wave that is not peaking. Your main aim is to get through the break with as much speed as possible.

You may need to sheet out at the top of the wave for an instant if the board feels as though it's going to jump — this lets the power off and you'll simply flop down the back.

So far I have talked about a wave of even height breaking nicely from left to right or vice versa. However, in northern Europe the waves don't present themselves so correctly. Most of the time they break in many different places at the same time, leaving peaks along their length. Trying to assess these sorts of wave is totally impractical because the waves never break in the same place at the same time (as they would do on a reef or point).

If things go wrong. . .

If things go wrong going out through the break a number of things could happen:

● You could be knocked down by a wave and chucked back up the beach.

● You could be knocked off by a wave but still be able to stand up.

● You could fall off and have to water-start. This usually happens when the wind drops and you are left to splash-down under the next big muncher that comes in.

Left: punching through the shore break. Accelerate, then luff up just before the white water so you meet the wave head on. Then bear away again for speed.

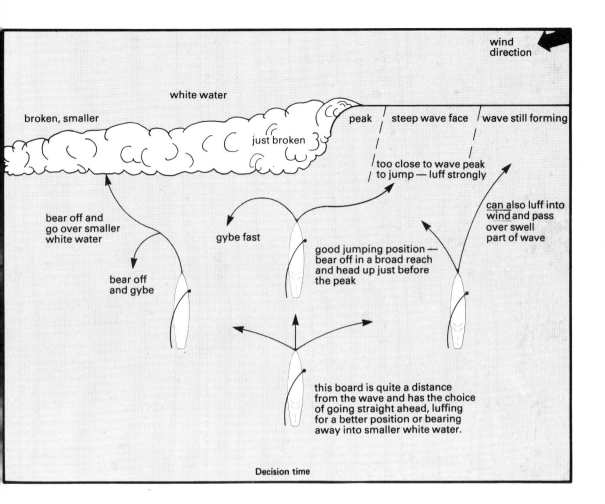

wind
direction

white water

broken, smaller

peak | steep wave face | wave still forming

just broken

too close to wave peak
to jump — luff strongly

bear off and
go over smaller
white water

can also luff into
wind and pass
over swell
part of wave

gybe fast

bear off
and gybe

good jumping position —
bear off in a broad reach
and head up just before
the peak

this board is quite a distance
from the wave and has the choice
of going straight ahead, luffing
for a better position or bearing
away into smaller white water.

Decision time

What can be done. If the wind does drop then pump like crazy to keep some momentum going and head for the lowest part of the wave. It's obviously better to fall off outside the area of breaking water. If you do fall off, immediately try to get into a water-start position ready for the wind to return. Failing that, either swim right away from the board and rig (but only if you are a competent swimmer and no more than twenty metres off the beach) or stay with your board and save your rig and yourself from breakage with a technique that is used by many of the top sailors in Hawaii: firstly, position yourself between the wave and the board and rig. Manoeuvre the rig so that the mast tip is facing the wave with you holding onto it and, as the wave peels over the top, dive under holding the tip of the mast as deep under the water as possible. This will allow the wave to pass over you and the rig, and you will act as an anchor under the water. Some sailors in Hawaii have a strap called a 'chicken loop' attached to the top of the sail which makes holding on rather easier while a ten-metre wall of water passes overhead. Once the wave has passed pull yourself hand over hand down the mast and proceed to water-start (described in chapter 7).

4 Wave jumping

The first thing to remember is that practically any board — be it open class racer or a sinker — can be jumped. The only thing that changes is the amount of control available to you. In the early days of windsurfing they were jumping boards very much like the stock board that most people sail in the flatboard class.

When I first started jumping it was also on one of these boards but without footstraps!

Jumping for beginners

Equipment. Equipment is very important when attempting your first jumps — a good strong mast, board and boom, along with a high-clewed sail, are essential (this is discussed in more detail in part 2).

A production board is a good way of starting, and polyethylene — being strong — makes many boards on today's market an ideal way to begin. As you become proficient you'll be more inclined towards a nice custom job which will probably be much shorter in length with less volume. It will also look good for the photographers! Masts come under the most pressure when jumping, especially when landing or wiping out, so choose a strong GRP mast which should also be quite stiff. Some sailors still use aluminium masts but they seem to be proving too weak for the job (though they are lighter).

You should own a couple of booms or an adjustable one (see chapter on rigging). Make sure they are nice and stiff — check this by flexing the whole boom: if there is more than 5 cm of play either way, it's probably not up to the job. To start with choose a board which is a floater — i.e. between 270 and 300 cm long (nine to ten feet). This will allow you to get airborne but will also allow you the volume for uphauling. Of course you will also need a good set of footstraps that are comfortable to sail with.

Wind direction. The direction of the wind determines the angle at which you will be hitting the waves. Generally a wind straight along the shoreline gives the best conditions for jumping — you can broad reach straight out into the waves and achieve maximum speed just before the jump. Try to avoid offshore winds at all costs. If the wind is coming over the land the water will generally be flat anyway.

Onshore winds can be very difficult, but if the wind is blowing onshore at an angle of about 45 degrees, jumping can be very good. You will need to gain plenty of speed on a broad reach and at the last moment head up to hit the wave peak bow first. If you have a choice of beaches then always go for the one where the wind is nearest to the side shore direction.

For beginners, pick a smaller wave to jump first. Then as you progress with good take-offs and landings you will want to jump higher and will automatically advance to the bigger stuff.

Practise hitting and jumping small 'walls' of white water to get the feel of things. Better still, why not try 'lake hopping', where you jump off the windblown chop?

Jumping your first wave — a long flat jump

OK, so you're ready to jump — what sort of jump are you going to try? To start with don't attempt anything too radical otherwise you'll end up breaking something. First try a long flat jump whereby you take off, have the board horizontal in flight and finally land tail first. Here's how to go about it.

1. Check your mast is in the rear position and the daggerboard is retracted.

2. Bear away towards the best part of the wave. Ideally you will be sailing on a broad reach at maximum speed.

3. As you approach the wave, make sure your

Below: take-off technique. Bear away for speed, sail up the 'ramp' and luff at the top. Take off straight-legged, then bend the knees to lift the back of the board.

feet are firmly in the footstraps and that you are unhooked from your harness.

4. As you hit the wave, simultaneously push your leeward rail down and lift the windward rail a little. This will turn the bottom of the board towards the wind slightly which will help your lift-off.

5. Aim the board in the direction that you want to go. As you leave the wave behind, crouch down and bend your legs, lifting the tail of the board clear of the water. You're now airborne, with the board parallel to the water.

6. While in the air control the rig as you would for normal sailing — you may find you need to sheet in a bit and lean the rig to windward.

7. Now you're coming in to land. All you have to do is to straighten your legs and this will ensure that you get a smooth tail-first landing. At the same time, sheet out the sail a little (if you keep it sheeted in you could go into a nose-dive). Once you have landed bend your knees to absorb the shock, sheet in again and sail off on a broad reach. Congratulations, you have just made your first jump!

To summarise, your main aim is to come out of the jump in one piece, with soft tail landings. From a three-metre jump, landing the board flat can be hard on your equipment and yourself. If you find

yourself out of control in the air simply let go of everything, get your feet out of straps and let go of the boom; the board will then keep going and you will fall. Usually the board and rig get blown downwind so that you will rarely get hurt, but it possible go down head-first into the water for safety's sake.

Advanced jumping

Different boards react differently in the air, so consider what sort of board you have before choosing a particular jump. For instance the longer type of funboard — up to 300 cm (9 to 10 feet) — will probably get greater distance and height because of the momentum gained before take off. But a sinker will get into radical upside-down positions quickly because of its lightness and small size.

Let's now take a look at what you can progress to. All the following jumps can be made from waves as small as a metre in height.

High flat jumps. These are much the same as the beginner's jump described earlier, except that you get more height before levelling off. To achieve this extra height bring your knees close into your body at the top of the jump; this will automatically level off the board in the air.

The photos above show take-off and landing from a different angle. Note how the legs are extended on landing so the tail is pushed down and lands first. On impact the legs are bent to absorb shock and the sail is sheeted in to regain speed. Below: advanced jumping — a high flat jump.

High vertical jumps. Broad reach out towards your wave, unhooked and comfortable in the straps. Focus your mind on the wave.

1. As with flat jumping, lift the windward rail with your front foot as you hit the wave.

2. Here's the difference: to get height, pull the sail towards the back of the wave and lean back over the board. Push the board forward with stretched legs at the same time exerting upward force with your feet.

3. Once you are in the air the sail should be raked right back over your body and kept there, while you move your legs and the board. The sail should act as a pivot, staying roughly in the same place all the time.

4. To come down simply sheet in to get the wind in the sail and to pull your body up. Careful, though — if you sheet in too early, the resulting nosedive can be both painful and expensive.

5. Once again, aim for a tail-first landing with legs slightly bent and ready for the impact of the board and water.

You will find eventually that the board simply becomes an extension of your feet in one brilliant triangle of energy!

Donkey kick. To achieve this jump, take off the wave and gain as much height as you can. Then kick the board out to one side with both legs stretched (hence the name 'donkey kick').

Table top. This is much the same as the 'donkey kick', the difference being that the board is turned upside down so the skegs face the sky. Once in the air, kick your legs out to one side and twist your body so the soles of your feet point skywards. The board will follow with its skegs upwards. Keep the rig horizontal. To land, reverse the procedure, i.e. pull your legs back in underneath you. This is a spectacular jump with a lot of twisting movement in the body, so you have to be flexible.

Upside down (tip dip). The upside-down 'tip dip' is one of the classic jumps, best executed by Robby Naish. The technique for getting into this position is much the same as the 'high vertical'

Opposite: a high vertical jump. Left: a 'tip dip'.

More advanced jumps. Top: a 'donkey kick'. Left: a 'table top'.

jump except that the legs and body must be shot off the top of the wave and at the same time the rig is pulled right back over your body to get the mast vertical. As the wave passes underneath you, you have enough height for the sail to be completely upside down with the tip buried in the wave.

Loop 360. At the time of writing no one has actually achieved a complete loop in the air, but some of the top Hawaiian sailors are getting 260 degrees. Prize money of some fifty thousand dollars is reputedly at stake for the man who is first captured on film doing a 360. The development of special loop rigs is taking place all the time and in years to come we will surely see somebody achieve this jump — without damaging themselves too much first.

5 Wave riding

Once you're well beyond the breaking waves and still heading out to sea, look for a good wave to ride back in. Choosing the right wave — one that won't break too early on you — comes with experience.

The *sets* of waves should be fairly obvious, especially if it's big stuff. If you want the biggest wave, and the best formed one, go for one in the middle of the set (say the third wave). But if you don't feel too confident then ride the last wave in the set. This means that if you muff it, or wipe out, you should have time to restart before the next set arrives.

Turning round

Having chosen your set, gybe in good time (see chapter 6) and sail along slowly, looking over your shoulder at the wave you want to ride. Check your daggerboard is up — it's almost impossible to control the board on a wave with the dagger down. If you've chosen, say, the third wave in the set let the first two pass underneath you by sheeting in and out to keep the board stalling, while still retaining enough speed to keep upright. As the third wave approaches, take a deep breath and prepare to do some ripping.

Basic wave riding

You have two objectives on the way in: to stay roughly on a broad reach, and to retain a good position on the wave — usually halfway up the face.

1. To catch the wave, increase your speed slightly by sheeting in about five to ten metres in front of it.

2. As the wave arrives it will pick up the back of the board. If the wind is light the forward speed of the board will be slower than the wave's so pump a few times to get going.

3. Now shift your weight forward by leaning forwards. This not only helps the board catch the wave but helps you keep your balance as the board accelerates down the face towards the trough.

4. Once you hit the trough at the bottom you'll want to get back onto the face, so turn the board slightly towards the wind without losing too much speed — but enough for the wave to catch up.

5. Sheet in and the whole process will start again.

If the wave becomes steep and cutting it's about to break. To avoid being caught in the middle of it bear away down the wave on a fast broad reach. The wave should now break behind you; be ready for a sudden gush of wind, especially on bigger waves, caused by the displacement of the air by the wave breaking. If you can, stay away from the white water because the turbulence caused by the air in the water decreases the amount of grip exerted by the skegs and board while you are sailing along. Consequently slide-outs and spin-outs occur.

Once the wave has broken your objective should either be to land (see chapter 8) or to gybe/tack out again. You must gain enough distance ahead of the white water that has broken behind you to give you time to gybe and be ready to punch through the same wave you've just ridden.

Once you have mastered staying on the wave, you're ready to try the whole range of surfing manoeuvres — 'cut backs', 'off the lips', etc.

Advanced riding techniques

For the best wave riding the wind direction should be side shore to slightly offshore and you should pick your wave so that its formation and height are both good.

The beginner will pick a quiet moment to turn and gybe before picking up the wave, but as you become more advanced you can gybe on the face of your chosen wave or better still off the lip; in other words you make your turn at the most spectacular time.

Here are some of the manoeuvres you can do on the face of the wave.

Cut back and roller-coaster.   The cut back is one of the simplest manoeuvres to perform once you're on the wave and sailing on a broad reach. Accelerate towards the bottom of the wave, then as you are just about to hit the trough turn into the wind by pulling the rig towards the back of the board. This will steer you back up the face (provided you have enough speed). Near the top of the wave push the rig forward quickly so you

1

2

3

1

2

3

Opposite: basic wave riding. Sheet out until the wave picks you up, then sheet in and steer to keep on its face.

This wave is dumping — so the sailor gains speed to pull ahead of it. Above: making a bottom turn.

bear away back down the face — this is the 'cut back'. Now link several cut backs together — this is a 'roller coaster'. Use your feet to help turn the board: dig in the windward rail with your front foot to turn out of the trough and depress the leeward rail with your back foot to help bear away as you hit the top of the wave. This basic manoeuvre can be done on any kind of footstrap board, but obviously the larger the board the slower the turns.

Bottom turn. The bottom turn is, as the name implies, a turn at the bottom of the wave. To achieve this you must have plenty of speed on the wave, with the wind directly cross-shore or slightly offshore. To begin with, bear down the wave face towards the bottom of the trough on a broad reach, then bear right away from the wind, moving along the bottom line of the wave. Your back foot will be depressing the leeward rail to carve you away from the wind and the rig should be sheeted out and pushed forward.

Off the lip. This is the natural lead-on from the bottom turn. Usually from the bottom of the wave you will bear back up the face, sheeted out and leaning forward with your weight still on the leeward rail. Once you are at the top of the wave transfer your weight to the windward rail. At the

29

Expert wave riding. The sailor makes a bottom turn (above), climbs the wave face (opposite) before carving off the lip (below). Note that the turns take him away from the white water.

same time sheet in and lean forward, carving the board back round and down the face of the wave. You should now be going in the same direction as before you made the bottom turn.

Jumping off the lip. This is another variation on the 'off the lip' manoeuvre. To attain the jump climb the face of the wave with plenty of speed. As you hit the top of the wave you can actually jump your board clear of the water. Once in the air, arrange the board and angle of flight so you land back on the same wave face! The idea is that when you come off the lip of the wave you make a low flat jump, twisting sideways so that the board is travelling along the wave. When you land, sheet in immediately and travel down the wave face. This is a very difficult manoeuvre and only a few of the stars are achieving success.

360 degrees on the wave. At the time of writing only two or three people in the world are successfully doing this incredible surfing manoeuvre. The turn makes an excellent end to a wave-riding routine. Try it *in front* of a small wave — *not* on a wave face. Essentially you stay on the same side of the sail throughout the manoeuvre and keep the same rail depressed the whole time, turning the board through 360 degrees. Note that the rig stays at the same angle to the board throughout the turn.

1. Sail on a fast broad reach and bear away.

2. When the board is pointing away from the wind push the rig into the wind. The board will gybe with you still on the 'old' side of the sail.

3. Keep the original rail depressed and keep turning. Raise the rig back and the board will tack with you still on the original side.

4. Finally, sheet in and go.

Above and right: a 'roller coaster' — ripping and slashing the wave while moving upwind.

Above: the great Robbie Naish jumping off the lip.

33

6 Gybing techniques

For each 'circuit' you make you will need to gybe twice — once out at sea when you turn round to ride the waves, and again near the beach when you want to gybe and punch out through the surf.

The flare gybe and the carve gybe are the two most important turning techniques: which one you choose is determined by the wind strength and the type of board you're riding. The difference between them is mainly that in a flare gybe the *windward* rail is depressed (as in normal longboard technique) while in a carve the *leeward* rail is depressed and the body leans into the turn (as you would on a surfboard or a bike). In a flare gybe the tail sinks somewhat, which naturally slows the board. On a sinker, particularly in light winds, this is tricky because the board may come to a stop and sink. Because of this I recommend:

On a long board use a flare gybe in lighter winds and a carve gybe in strong winds.

On a short board use a carve gybe throughout.

General advice

After mastering the flare and the carve gybe there are many variations you can try — of which more later. But for *any* gybe:

● Check the daggerboard is fully retracted before you begin.

● Choose your bit of water carefully — make you offshore turn outside the wave sets and you inshore gybe ahead of a wave. And practise on lake first!

● If you're moving very fast, slow down to reasonable speed before you begin.

● Having decided to gybe, go for it.

Carve gybe

Let's say you want to turn to the right (see photo sequence).

1. Sailing on a broad reach check your daggerboard is retracted and unhook your harness.

2. Take your back foot out of its strap and press down on the *leeward* rail. Lift up the windward rail with your front foot (still in the strap). Lean into the turn and keep the sail sheeted in.

3. Hold this position so the board turns through the wind to a clew-first position. Note that the angle of the rig relative to the wind has not changed.

4. Now take your front foot out of the strap and push it into the new back strap.

5. Transfer your right hand to the mast and let the clew of the sail swing round.

6. Let go with your left hand and transfer it to the new side of the boom.

7. Finally let go of the mast with your right hand, grab the boom, put your front foot in the strap and sheet in.

8. If the board seems to be turning too far, push the sail forwards to stop it.

Below: the author demonstrating a carve gybe. Right: the classic position halfway through a carve gybe.

Flare gybe

Once again, I'm assuming you want to gybe to the right (see photo sequence).

1. Unhook while sailing on a broad reach.

2. Take your left foot out of its strap and move it back and to the windward side of the board. Take your right foot out and move it forwards slightly.

3. Put most of your weight on your left foot (on the windward rail). The tail of the board will sink and the nose will flare up (hence the name) and around.

4. Keep your body upright and the sail full of wind. The board turns 'on itself' very quickly to a clew-first position.

5. Now push your left foot into the new back strap.

6. Transfer your right hand to the mast and let the clew of the sail swing round.

7. Let go with your left hand and transfer it to the new side of the boom.

8. Finally let go of the mast with your right hand, grab the boom, put your front foot in the strap and sheet in.

Duck gybe

The board turns more quickly in a duck gybe than in a carve gybe. It also retains more speed because the sail only goes clew-first for an instant. This time the photo sequence shows a turn to the left.

1. As in a carve gybe depress the leeward rail and lean into the turn.

2. As the board points away from the wind transfer your right hand to the back of the boom and pull the clew of the sail across your body.

3. At the same time let go with your left hand

duck under the sail and grab the boom on the new side.

4. Finally transfer your right hand to the boom. Continue to depress the left-hand rail to carve the board through the turn. Sheet in as it carves round and sail off.

Once you have mastered the duck gybe technique you might want to try some variations.

One-handed duck gybe (turning to the left). As you duck under the boom lean over to the left and dip your left hand in the water. The idea is that the board pivots around this hand — you then quickly transfer your left hand to the boom before completing the turn.

Foot-of-sail duck gybe. Some people find this variation easier to do than the ordinary boom-to-boom transition. The difference is that when you cross your front hand over your back hand you grab the foot of the sail instead of the boom.

Above: a flare gybe. Note how the nose of the board flares up and around as the windward rail is depressed.

Below: a duck gybe. In lighter winds (as here) the duck can be made early.

Above: tacking

Tacking

For the larger types of funboards it might be that you are nervous about gybing and would rather do a quick tack. Also, you sometimes drop downwind and need to beat back; gybing at the end of each leg would lose ground to windward so the ability to tack is useful. Of course, you can't tack a sinker.

As in the photo sequence I'm assuming you're turning to the right:

1. Rake the rig back to turn the board towards the wind.

2. Transfer your right hand to the mast just below the boom.

3. As the board turns through the eye of the wind transfer your left hand to the mast and jump around to the new side using the mast as a pivot.

4. As you land on the new side grab the boom with your right hand and sheet in quickly to prevent the waves knocking you off-balance. Use your feet to balance the board too.

5. Transfer your left hand to the boom and push the rig well forwards to help complete the turn.

7 Water-starting

One of the most important aspects of wave sailing is to know how to water-start in light or strong winds, and on flat or rough water.

The type of board you are riding will dictate whether you water-start all the time, or uphaul. Because of their lack of volume, sinkers have to be water-started every time, whereas a marginal floater can be both uphauled (with difficulty) or water-started. It is normally easier to practise with a longer board so that if you get too tired you can uphaul it. Once you've mastered the technique, however, I would recommend water-starting even with floaters because uphauling in wind and waves can be exhausting.

Aligning the board and rig

When you wipe out it is very rare that the board and rig are in the perfect position for water-starting. So your first job is to manipulate them into what I will call the starting position (see diagram overleaf). Depending on how you fall, you may find:

- You need to spin the board around (to face in the opposite direction).

- You need to swim the rig around to the other side of the board.

- You need to flip the rig so the luff of the sail faces the wind. Sometimes you will have to do all three!

Below: water-starting.

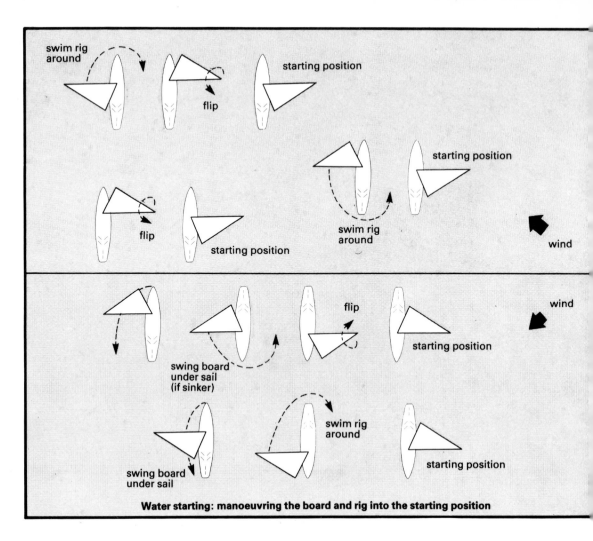

swim rig around

flip

starting position

starting position

flip

starting position

swim rig around

wind

wind

swing board under sail (if sinker)

flip

starting position

swim rig around

swing board under sail

starting position

Water starting: manoeuvring the board and rig into the starting position

Turning the board around

If you're sailing a short board take one end of the board and push it under water and under the sail (usually it's easier to take the bow because it has less buoyancy). Meanwhile you stay to windward of the board and rig.

If you're on a long board leave the board and concentrate on the rig.

Swimming the sail around

Hold the mast just above the boom and lever it around the board. It helps to push your end of the board under water.

Always lead with the mast side of the sail — otherwise the clew will dig into the water.

Flipping the rig

Make your way to the clew end of the boom. Tread water and push up on the boom until the wind catches the sail and flips it over. Slide your hand down the boom as it flips to slow it down, otherwise it may go under the water on the new side which will make raising the rig harder.

Below: a strong-wind water-start. Note how I use the swell passing under my body to help lift me clear of the water.

Water-starting in strong winds

Firstly get into the starting position.

1. Swim to the tip of the mast and push the tip so that it is out of the water. The wind should help you here by flowing under the sail and helping to lift it.

2. Still treading water, 'walk' along the mast hand-over-hand lifting the mast clear of the water until you get to the boom. Beware at this point of showing too much sail area to the wind, or the rig will flip and you will have to start again.

3. Once you have reached the boom, push up the sail so that excess water drains off towards the clew of the sail.

4. At this point, you should still be treading water. Align the board on a broad reach by moving the rig (which is now clear of the water) towards the back or front of the board. This is the same steering technique that you use in normal sailing.

5. Pull yourself up closer to the board and get your back foot in the back strap. Hoist the sail a little higher until the wind lifts you out of the water. You can help by pumping the sail and treading water with your front foot. Once up, put your front foot in the front strap and sail off.

Hints.
● Don't let the board head too much downwind, because once you hoist the sail you will fly out of the water very quickly and lose control. Alternatively don't let the board luff up into the wind while you are in the water.

● A short boom and high-aspect sail make water-starting much less effort.

Water-starting in light and gusty winds

Many people are criticised, quite rightly, when they venture out to sea with semi-sinker funboards in winds that are dropping or very light. The inevitable rescues are bad publicity for our sport. The problem is that once the wind has dropped and the sailor falls in, the wind is too light to pull him back out again.

Since the light-wind water-start is tricky it is a good idea to practise it on a lake with the wind gusting between two and four.

Firstly get into the usual starting position.

1. Align the board on a broad reach, 'walk' down the mast to the boom and hoist the sail out of the water. Remember, without much wind around more effort will be required to push the sail out.

2. Once your hands are on the boom, lift the sail as high as possible. Drop your front hand onto the mast, about halfway between board and boom.

3. Still keeping the board on a broad reach get your back foot in between the back straps and the front straps. (If you have your foot too far back, it will unbalance the board when you are up and moving.)

4. At the same time, bring your body in closer to the board and pump with your front leg to help hoist you out of the water.

5. Push the sail as upright as is possible to catch the wind and from here pump the sail to pull you up. At the same time bend your back leg and step onto the board with your front leg, balancing and pumping the sail to gain speed.

6. Finally, move your front hand from the mast back onto the boom.

Hints.
● Watch out for gusts, they will obviously help you.
● When holding the boom and mast be careful that you don't sheet the rig in too much, since this can sometimes swing the board into the wind (because the rig is positioned towards the back of the board). To solve this problem push the rig as far forwards as you can and keep it as upright as possible.

Water-starting in swell and waves

If the waves are not too big, or you have fallen off outside the break, the best time to be pulled out of the water is when the swell passes underneath your body. You are, naturally, lifted slightly out of the water and therefore that much closer to sailing again. The sail is also working in cleaner air at the crest of the wave (there's much less wind in the trough).

Uphauling

Uphauling a marginal sinker is difficult but you may have to do it if there's not enough wind to water-start.

The problem is balancing the board because the bow or stern tend to sink. So stand with your feet wide apart, one each side of the mast.

8 Coming ashore

ou're lucky if you can land on a gently shelving
each. All too often the shore shelves steeply,
esulting in a vicious shore break. However,
ou've got to land sometime, and I'll try to show
ou how to avoid getting munched on your way in.
The secret of successful landing is being in the
ght place at the right time. Usually it's best to ride
on the back of a wave and sail up the beach just
ehind the white water. There are two ways of
etting onto the back of a wave:

You can drop off the wave you are riding by
ecreasing your speed, i.e. by sheeting out and
lowing down. This allows the wave to overtake
ou; as it passes, sheet in again and ride in on the
ack.

● Alternatively increase your speed by bearing
away and catching up with the wave that is ahead
of you.

As you follow the wave in and approach the
beach, remember to unhook your harness and
step out of the footstraps. Then if anything
untoward happens, at least you won't get caught
up with your rig and board.

Landing on a short board

1. When you judge the water to be knee deep,
step off, transferring your front hand to the mast.

2. Grab the back footstrap with your back hand
and lift the board and rig into the air.

3. Run up the beach.

Below: landing a short board.

Above: landing a long board.

Finally, if things go wrong (they're bound to sometimes) and you get caught in the shore break:

● If you're in waist-high water (or deeper), save your rig by grabbing the top of the mast and burying it under the water so the waves pass over the rig rather than through it. Let the wave pass, water-start and sail in.

● If you're in shallow water, pick up the board and rig and run up the beach.

Landing on a long board

If the board is too long and heavy to lift out of the water:

1. Jump off.

2. Transfer your front hand to the mast.

3. Grab the back strap and push the board up the beach.

Alternatively wrap your arm round the back of the board and push it up the beach on the rail. The rig is held clear in each case by your front hand on the mast.

Hints

● Don't jump in too early, because if you are up to your waist in water you won't be able to get ashore before the next big wave eats you!

● Conversely, don't jump off too late or the board will get damaged in shallow water. Don't sail too far on the back of the wave, as you may overtake it or get caught on the crest as it breaks which will throw you off.

● Avoid groynes and the water surrounding them at all costs. Sometimes groynes create their own mini rip currents, which can catch you and result in serious damage.

● Take care to organise your rig and board properly on the beach (i.e. nose and mast side of sail pointing into the wind) so that the wind doesn't pick the sail up and smash the lot.

Part 2
Background

9 Wind and wave theory

Let's look at the characteristics of each wind direction shown in the diagram below.

1 Wind onshore

Fairly safe. Beating out is difficult, especially in light winds. Waves tend to dump. Wave riding is fair, but you have to bear off the whole time. Usually a consistent wind.

2 Wind side/onshore

With the wind in this direction it's easier to get out through the break, and wave jumping is fairly good. Wave riding is OK, but there is a tendency for inexperienced people to get blown downwind. A fairly consistent wind.

3 Wind side shore

The best direction. It is easy to get out, wave riding and jumping are good but the wind may be patchy, especially if it's shifting slightly offshore. The inexperienced will be blown right downwind.

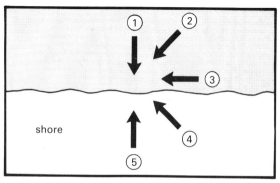

4 Wind side/offshore

This direction is still good for wave riding and jumping. This wind will hold the waves up more. Bad news for beginners or the inexperienced — who could be blown out to sea.

5 Wind offshore

Not very good for anything and definitely bad for beginners and the inexperienced. Only experienced wave sailors should sail in these conditions.

Cliffs and headlands

The figure opposite shows what happens when the wind is affected by cliffs. The bay, let's say, is 5 kilometres long, with high cliffs at either end. I've also added some rocks and currents just to make things more interesting.

In area A the wind has to lift over the cliff or swing round it. This leaves a large turbulent area just under the cliff, with the wind increasing as you get further away from it. Area A will also have heavy currents taking you out around the headlands. Area B will be calm because of the sheltering effect of the other cliffs. If you launch in A or B you will make things very difficult for yourself and would do better to set off from the middle of the bay.

Area C will be a good sailing area with fairly safe side-shore winds, some good waves and unaffected air flow.

Area D is known as an overfall. This is where an underwater shelf or band of rock rises suddenly to create two different depths of water. The effect

Above: sailing at Hookipa on Maui — world-famous for its waves. The reef ensures a constant and predictable break.

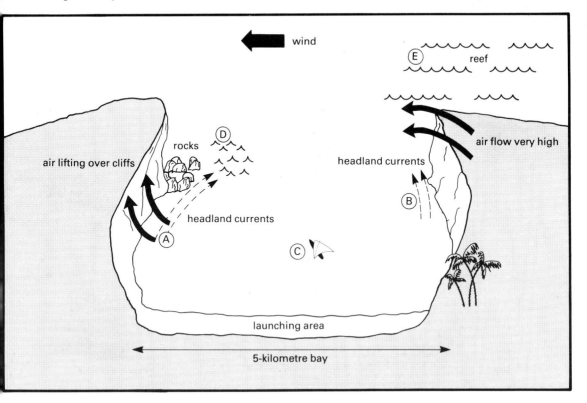

wind

E reef

air lifting over cliffs

rocks

D

air flow very high

headland currents

headland currents

A

B

C

launching area

5-kilometre bay

on the surface can be quite dramatic. This can occur in the open sea, but is most commonly found around headlands and cliffs. What happens is that the currents deep in the water suddenly hit the rocks and have nowhere to go but up towards the surface. The ensuing chaos on top of the water resembles short, tight pinnacle waves, which stand very upright. They are bumpy to sail on, and these areas are generally to be avoided.

The reef break on the opposite side of the bay (E) is where there is a gradual rise in rock (or coral) level. The water level then has to build up over this and in doing so creates waves that are good to ride and jump. These waves are generally far better than a shore break because they are uniform. After the waves pass over the reef and reach deep water they settle down again.

The diagram below shows a headland with a point break. Sail out through the undisturbed water in areas X and Z, or through the deep-water channel Y. Ride the waves back over either reef.

Different types of waves

For many surfers and boardsailors the ultimate waves are to be found in Hawaii and Australia. The waves can build up to enormous proportions especially after storms at sea, sometimes being 10 to 15 metres high. The rest of us, though, sail in waves that are a good deal smaller and a good deal messier, i.e. there is no set pattern to which way the wave breaks or just where it is going to break.

A good breaking wave will peel either left or right, depending on the type of break. Once again it's usually a lot more consistent when the wave comes from very deep water and builds up over a shallow area of coral, sand or rock. If you imagine yourself coming in on the wave and the breaking white water is on your left, the wave is called a right-hand break. A wave with a left-hand break has the white water to your right.

A wave builds up in height and force as it travels so you can expect bigger waves on a beach which has a large mass of water in front of it. In Hawaii for instance, waves generated by storms some 3000 kilometres away in the Pacific have no land mass in the way to prevent them reaching the Islands. Whereas if you live, say, on the northern coast of France or the south coast of Britain, you will find waves that have travelled only about 100 kilometres and are mushy and irregular as a result. This chop will have low spots and peaks which rise and drop irregularly.

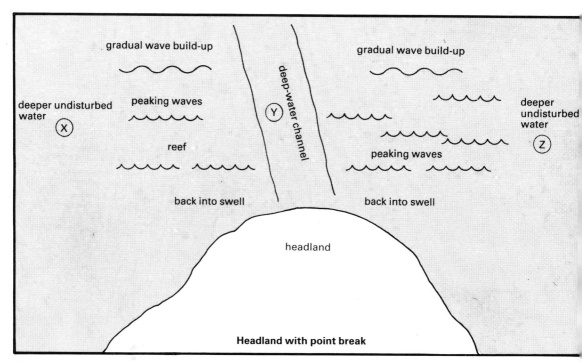

Headland with point break

10 Equipment

In most boardsailing shops there's a bewildering variety of funboards and rigs. The aim of this chapter is to help you choose gear that will suit your needs: it should give you some ammunition to deal with all the slick sales-talk, as well as keeping you on speaking terms with your bank manager.

Sails

In chapter 1 I talked about the ideal *size* (in square feet or square metres) for a sail. I want to look here at the *design* (or shape) of the sail. The diagram below shows three variations on the shape of a 4.9 m² sail. Note that wave sails should all be cut very flat to keep the centre of effort forward and make the rig manageable.

Pinhead. The pinhead is ideal for strong winds and flat water because the leech is hollow and the power point (marked with an x) is well forward. This prevents the board slewing up into the wind. In waves the long boom can be a problem when water-starting and when making bottom turns (see 'wave riding').

Fathead. By putting the area at the top the sail-maker can produce a tall narrow sail, set on a very short boom. This is extremely useful in large waves. In light winds and swell it's useful to have the area high up to catch clean wind above the

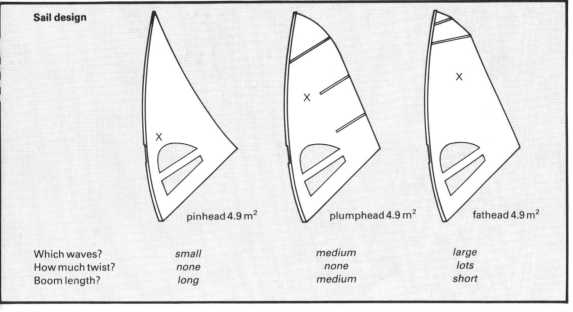

Sail design

pinhead 4.9 m²	plumphead 4.9 m²	fathead 4.9 m²

	pinhead 4.9 m²	plumphead 4.9 m²	fathead 4.9 m²
Which waves?	small	medium	large
How much twist?	none	none	lots
Boom length?	long	medium	short

wave crests. The problem is that in stronger winds the top twists off which makes the rig less controllable.

Plumphead. This design is a good compromise between the two extremes.

Masts

Aluminium masts are light, but won't stand much battering — so use an epoxy or glassfibre mast which is quite stiff. If the sail twists off too much at the top or creases badly the mast is probably too floppy. You may be able to cure this by cutting the top 25 centimetres (10 inches) off the mast and making up the length with a mast extension at the bottom. Reinforce your mast with fibreglass around the bottom and where the boom goes. Always make sure that your mast is sealed at both ends; this is because it is very difficult to water-start with a mast full of sea.

Mast extension

A mast extension which can be adjusted is of great benefit to the high-wind sailor. The extension raises the whole rig up into the air, thereby keeping the clew and boom well clear of the water; ideally the tack of the sail should be at least 30 centimetres (12 inches) from the board. An adjustable extension also allows you to 'fine tune' the height of your boom.

The extension should fit into the mast without any sloppiness. If it is too loose there will be leverage on the mast, which might crack around the base after a heavy landing from a jump or a wipe-out.

Below: an adjustable mast track. Use the front position for beating and move it back downwind.

Boom

Make sure your boom has good solid ends which aren't liable to snap on impact on the first jump. Make sure it is also stiff. To test this try pulling each side of the boom apart: if there is more than 5 centimetres (2 inches) of give, it is probably too flexible. Make sure that the boom has a good shape; a narrow boom will fit a flat sail much better than a wide one. A good boom for wave sailing will be between 1.8 m and 2.3 m long. This length allows the boom to stay totally clear of the waves when riding, and also makes trimming the sail easier and neater. The main advantage of having a boom made to fit the sail is that you get a better response when sailing.

Other parts of the rig

The lines that tie your rig together should be nice and long, and pre-stretched so that everything can be tied off without having to worry about whether it's going to break or come undone out at sea.

Power joints (universal joints) are becoming better made. Many people now use the Urethane power joints which are virtually indestructible. The more sophisticated have wire running through the rubber, so that even if the rubber breaks the wire will be least hold the ends together while you make your way back to the beach. Remember also, to attach your safety leash so it cannot get wound around the power joint.

Boards

There are three categories of high-wind boards. A *floater* is a board that supports an 80-kg man and

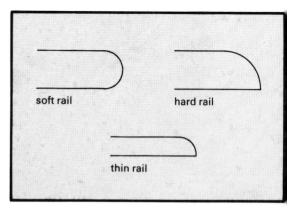

that can be uphauled with ease — in this book these are termed 'long boards'. Next comes the *marginal floater*; it won't sink under your weight, but when uphauling you will have to balance it with your legs wide apart. For the average man this board is usually about 2.8 m long. Finally the *sinker*; this is your out-and-out low-volume board built for winds over force 4 — in lighter winds it will sink under your weight. Sinkers must be water-started or beach started, whereas the floaters and marginal floaters can both be up-hauled if need be.

In general the shorter and narrower a board is, the more manoeuvrable it becomes. The wider a board is, the more stable it becomes. If the wide point is well back, the board will be quick to plane; this sort of board is ideal in a force 3 to 4 wind strength, but in stronger winds the tendency is for the board to bounce and skip, especially in chop, and so responsiveness and control when manoeuvring will suffer. Boards that are wide in the tail need more fins.

If the tail of the board is narrow, it takes longer to get planing but turns well. Only small skegs are needed because the narrow tail holds the water well.

Rail shapes. The shape of the rail (edge of the board) is important in determining how the board turns. Firstly look at the rail towards the back of the board. If it is soft (rounded) the board will skid during a turn, while a hard rail will grip the water and help you turn tightly. Thin rails also help turning because they reduce buoyancy and allow the tail to sink more easily. Of course this makes the board unsuitable for light winds!

Towards the bow the rails should be soft — the last thing you want is the bow digging in and stopping you turning.

Bottom shapes. The board should generally be rounded at the bow and with a V-shape towards the stern. With hard rails, this V helps turning and foot steering, and gives the board more grip on the water — which is useful when beating. The only problem is that you need more wind to start planing.

Tail shapes. A narrow tail (such as a pintail) is good for carving tight turns since it grips the water — this is ideal for wave riding. The only problem is that it lacks volume, so it's hard to jump with a narrow tail — the back of the board slices through the wave on take-off instead of being pushed into the air. The swallowtail is one compromise; when flat it has volume, but when banked during a turn one of the tails comes out of the water giving a pintail effect. Wings are also useful in giving a good grip at the back without sacrificing too much volume. So wings aid jumping because they keep width near the tail.

Skegs

Skegs are used to help the board sail in a straight line and to prevent spin-out — that nasty feeling when the tail of the board suddenly whips out to one side. If you find your board sliding or spinning out, either after a high jump or at high speed, the only way to resolve the trouble while sailing along is to slow down by sheeting out and flick the board from side to side by depressing heel and then toe in the back strap. This will help shift the small pocket of air trapped around the skegs that is

Below: These side skegs are toed-in to aid turning ability.

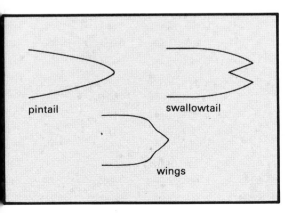

pintail   swallowtail

wings

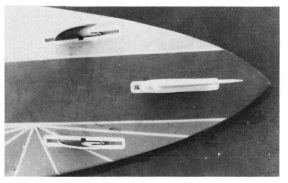

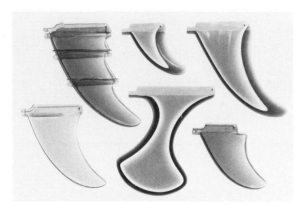

Above: skegs come in all shapes and sizes. Note the fences on the top left skeg.

causing the problem — known as 'cavitation'.

Some boards have a single skeg: make sure it has enough area to make the board perform. Others have a 'thruster' arrangement with two small skegs grouped around a larger one. Note that the small skegs are often 'toed-in' towards the front of the board. The idea is that when the board turns one side is dug into the water exposing one skeg (which does nothing) and putting pressure on the other (because this is set at an angle it helps the board turn). If the side skegs are too big all three will bite during a turn and the manoeuvre will be sloppy.

Whether you have a single skeg or a set that looks like a school of sharks, small adjustments will make a difference to performance. So:

● If you find you are skipping out in chop with a single skeg, try a bigger one.

● If cavitation takes place with a three-fin arrangement, the fins may be too close together, or the winger skegs too big. You could change to an anti-cavitation fence fin — they do work.

● To make small sinkers tighter in the turn, have the three-fin arrangement pushed close together towards the back of the board. To make it looser in the turn (i.e. to make nice long arcs when carve gybing) move the side fins further forward and leave the back one where it is. What you are effectively doing is widening the gap between the back skeg and the two smaller skegs, creating less drag in the gybe.

11 Safety

Of all the chapters in the book, this is probably the most important one. To be able to sail in safety without endangering your life or others should be uppermost in your mind every time you go out. Here are some simple do's and don'ts.

DO. . .

. . . check the weather forecast.
. . . know how to swim.
. . . carry plenty of spare lines.
. . . tell someone that you are going out, and when you're going.
. . . practise self-rescue.
. . . learn the right-of-way rules for ordinary sailing/wave sailing.
. . . find — and keep within — your limitations.
. . . wear a buoyancy aid and carry flares.
. . . check that your sail is the right size for the wind strength.
. . . check that your gear is in good order before going sailing.
. . . make sure your leash works.

DON'T. . .

DON'T go out in offshore winds, unless rescue facilities are at hand.
DON'T go out without a wetsuit or adequate covering from the elements.
DON'T carry on too long. When you feel tired, pack up and go home
DON'T abandon your board and try to swim for it — *ever*.
DON'T go out in heavy rip currents.
DON'T bug surfers, they have as much right to the waves as you have.

DON'T sail upwind of obstructions like piers and rocks. The wind will lift up, leaving a calm patch. DON'T go out alone.

Rules of the road

When a crowd of people is sailing in high winds and waves, things can become exceptionally dangerous with boards (and people) flying around all over the place. So a few basic safety rules should be learnt and respected.

1. The boardsailor riding a wave towards the shore has right of way over someone going out through the sets. B in the diagram below must give way to A.

2. The boardsailor nearest the breaking section of the wave has right of way. D must give way to C.

3. The boardsailor riding the wave furthest from the shore has right of way. A must give way to D.

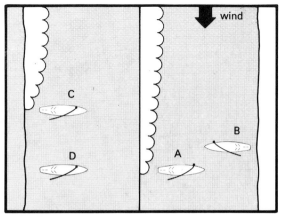

4. Give way to surfers at all times (you have more manoeuvrability than they do).

5. Always look around before gybing to make sure no one is sailing on the blind side of your sail — a nasty accident could result.

Have fun on the waves but keep well out of the way and steer clear of other people. *They* might not know the rules.

Self rescue

If you suddenly find yourself overcome by the conditions, or your gear breaks, don't waste time and energy trying to sail back. If there's another sailor around, ask him or her to help you. Alternatively attract attention on shore by waving your arms in the international distress signal. They may be able to get a rescue board out or help you rescue yourself. If there's no one around, adopt the following self-rescue technique:

1. Take the mast foot out of the board and undo the mast leash. Sit across the board and push the rig away until you're holding the clew of the sail.

2. Undo one side of the outhaul, take out the battens and roll the sail towards the mast as tightly as possible (you can roll the battens inside the sail).

3. The boom is still attached to the mast by the inhaul. Align the boom along the mast with the end of the boom near the mast tip. Use the outhaul to tie the boom to the mast and to lash the rolled-up sail to the mast.

4. Use the uphaul rope to lash the sail at the other end of the mast.

5. Use any spare pieces of line or harness lines to strap the rig to the board. If it is a long board then lengthways is probably better, but on a short board lay the rolled-up rig across the middle of the board.

6. Paddling is difficult and tiring. Try to find the most comfortable position, but always sit or lie on top of the rig. If you're really in trouble dump the rig — you will be able to paddle faster without it.

7. Remember — never leave your board.

Right: self-rescue. For short boards it's better to paddle with the rig across the middle of the board.

54

Above: wave-sailing is a dangerous sport. Where the waves are biggest the landing can be treacherous, like these rocks at Hookipa.

Rescuing another sailor

Get the victim to furl his rig as described above. Then sail up to leeward of his board and get him to grab your mast foot with one hand and hook a foot over the back of your board. In this way you can sail slowly back to shore towing him alongside.

Reefing your sail

Another way to help yourself when in trouble is to reef your sail. You can cut down the sail area by about thirty per cent in this way and it could be enough to get you home safely. Try it on the beach or at home so that you know exactly what is involved.

Method 1. Slacken the outhaul and downhaul and roll the top half of the sail around the mast. It should stay in position.

Method 2. The method I favour, having used it in a strong mistral in the south of France, is to take a length of rope and then grab the top metre or so of sail and lash it tightly to the mast. You have then decreased the sail area effectively and quickly.

Safety leashes

The safety leash should be attached to the nose of the board. When the rig and board are separated in waves the leash from the mast foot will keep the board nose-to-wave with the rig acting as a sea anchor, preventing the rig and board from going anywhere.

Safety accessories

Flares. Go out and buy a couple of flares for sea sailing — few boardsailors even think of carrying something like this. They are cheap and easy to use and sail with. Carry them either in the base of your mast or strapped to the boom. The life expectancy of a flare is about two-and-a-half to three years. Make sure the ones you buy are fully waterproof.

Harnesses. There are many new quick-release hooks on the market and most of them now use

Top: the international distress signal. Above: first-aid for a broken boom.

the 'V' hook which is virtually non-'snagable'. Always use a buoyancy harness of the kind that will give you some support when in the water.

Hypothermia

Much has been written in journals and publications on hypothermia, and rightly so. The majority of winter rescues end with the guy on the board being carted off to hospital with hypothermia well set in. It can be a killer, and so all boardsailors should take real note and know exactly what to look out for.

Symptoms. Hypothermia, to put it fairly simply, is when the inner core of the torso falls considerably in temperature to around 35 degrees C (95-96 degrees F). This is too cold a temperature for the bodily functions to continue to operate satisfactorily, and so recognisable symptoms begin to appear. Firstly, you will be shivering and feeling very cold; so don't hesitate to get ashore and home to warm yourself up. If it becomes serious (and this can happen very quickly) the symptoms will be a lack of interest in what is going on, slow reactions, confusion and slurred speech; also numbness and cramping of muscles can result.

What can be done? If you find you have to help out on the beach when someone has been brought in, the first thing to remember is to shelter the victim from the wind, otherwise his body temperature will continue to fall.

The patient must then be warmed up, and this is where problems can arise. Rewarming must be done under medical supervision — so summon an ambulance, and concentrate on preventing any further drop in body temperature. Get the patient into a sheltered position, preferably in a warm atmosphere, and wrap him up in plenty of blankets. Don't do anything that might bring blood up to the skin surface (thus cooling it further) such as rubbing limbs, applying a hot-water bottle, or making the patient exercise. Give a hot drink if the patient is conscious, but NEVER give alcohol.

If the patient is unconscious he must be placed in the recovery position, and if he is not breathing then resuscitation methods must be used (see any first-aid manual).

The vital things to remember are to keep the patient insulated, keep him absolutely still, and to seek medical advice *even if the patient appears to make a quick recovery.*

Part 3
Winning in waves

12 Wave competitions

There are several sorts of competitions designed for high winds and big waves. Most of these are speed races (man-on-man) but the most spectacular event is the wave riding and jumping competition, which is judged on points.

Wave riding and jumping

Competitors start out to sea and have 15 minutes to show off their routine, doing tricks as they ride in and jumping as they go out. Each person can make as many circuits as he likes in the time allowed. The top sailors have several rigs and boards on shore; if something breaks or conditions change they can sail in and change gear. Caddies are allowed too — they can sail out with new gear if the competitor is stranded at sea. Of course, while all this is going on time (and therefore points) is being lost.

Below: early rounds in wave performance contests feature several boards at a time. Final rounds are man-on-man.

How is it judged? At the time of writing there is no single, internationally accepted set of rules. But roughly speaking one-third of the points are awarded for wave riding, one-third for jumping and one-third for the transitions.

Personally I would like to see wave *riding* judged in the same way as surfing competitions, where each rider is allowed ten waves and is judged on the best four. In surfing competitions "the surfer who attains the longest and most radical ride on the most critical section of the biggest wave shall be deemed the winner". That seems fair enough for us, too.

squash tail

classic pintail

World Cup board

wave board

production board

custom board

ins & outs
and slalom

round tail with wings

pintail with double wings

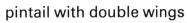

Ten out of ten — maximum score for a perfect wave performance. The sailor heads towards the shore in a trough. He bears away from the wind, then carves back off the top of the white water down the face. After working the wave to the max, he moves ahead of it giving himself enough time to duck gybe and sail out through what is left of the same wave. He picks up speed and heads for the peak of the next wave, making a high flat jump and landing perfectly to continue his routine.

The wave *jumping* is (and should be) judged rather like ice skating with points for height and length of jumps plus points for style — i.e. how radical the jump was.

Advice on your routine. Check the competition rules carefully and try to determine how the scoring will be done. Do plenty of limbering up before you go afloat and then only do tricks you are 95 per cent certain will come off. Do the easiest tricks first to gain confidence (and points), leaving the harder tricks till later, and try not to fall — wasted time means wasted points.

Your sequence of tricks must flow — the end of one trick should leave you well placed to begin the next. Practise your routine in segments; then put all the segments together to make the whole show.

Practise in all conditions. In a blow, the tricks happen so fast you may run out of things to do before the fifteen minutes are up — so take your time. Concentrate on the easier tricks. In less wind your routine tends to look dull, so pack in the action even if it means repeating tricks several times.

If you are a beginner, work out a sequence and stick to it. If you are more experienced, plan the first half and then improvise until the end. In this way you can amass plenty of points early on, and are then free to exploit wind and wave conditions to the full.

Equipment. Only use gear you're 100 per cent confident will work in the prevailing conditions. Have longer/shorter boards and bigger/smaller rigs onshore in case the wind changes — watch out, for example, for gusty winds when a very short board and small sail will not support you in the lulls.

Slalom and 'ins and outs'

These events are races held in the surf. Courses vary tremendously, but in slalom competitions the emphasis is on turning, whereas in 'ins and outs' speed is the main criterion.

Giant slalom. Usually there is a Le Mans start between two poles on shore. All the competitors may start together, or they may go off in pairs with the winner going through to the next heat. A typical course is shown opposite.

Choose a fast reaching board that gybes well and practise tight carve gybes for the turns. You will also need flare gybes if you round in close company.

Below: the start of a Pan Am World Cup race in Hawaii — the trophy that everyone wants to win.

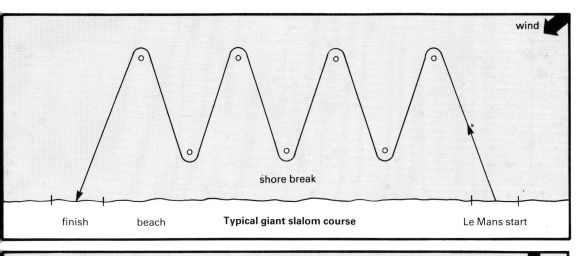

Typical giant slalom course

wind

finish   beach   shore break   Le Mans start

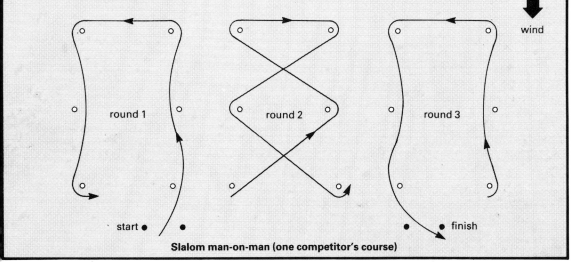

round 1   round 2   round 3

wind

start ●   ●   ●   ● finish

Slalom man-on-man (one competitor's course)

Slalom man-on-man. Competitors sail in pairs, each going round the course in *opposite directions*. There is a timed countdown through the startline, then rounds 1, 2 and 3 (see diagram above) are sailed. The winner is the first person through the finish.

Choose a board with a retractable dagger, since the course contains several beats.

'Ins and outs'. 'Ins and outs' courses feature Le Mans starts followed by plenty of fast reaching. The course shown (right) has no beat but other varieties do — so you may need a board with a retractable dagger.

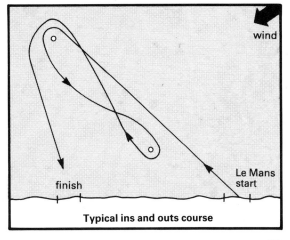

wind

finish   Le Mans start

Typical ins and outs course

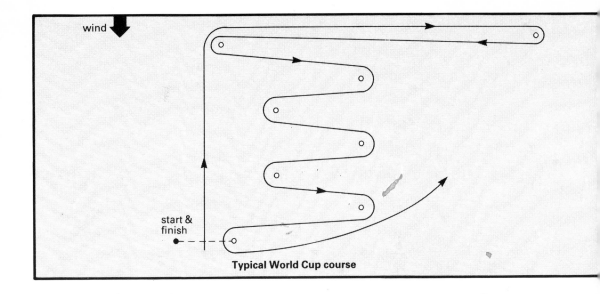

wind

start & finish

Typical World Cup course

World Cup racing

World Cup racing is similar to triangle racing but with the emphasis on high winds and reaching. Extra gybes are often built in to test the skill of the sailors still further.

Use a long, fast planing board — similar to a normal racing board but with a narrower tail and slightly less width (and therefore less volume). It should have a fully retracting and easy-to-operate daggerboard system, plus a sliding mast track which can be adjusted easily while sailing. This allows you to push the rig to the front of the track for upwind work, which increases speed through better control and board handling. To go downwind slide the rig towards the back of the track for quicker planing. The board should also be equipped with plenty of footstraps — positioned both for upwind and downwind work.

Tactics for triangle racing are fully covered in the companion volume *Board Racing* by Geoff Turner and Tim Davison.